E-business

HELPING DIRECTORS TO UNDERSTAND AND EMBRACE THE DIGITAL AGE

Editor, Director Publications: Tom Nash
Managing Editor: Lesley Shutte
Consulting Editor: Professor Jim Norton
Production Manager: Victoria Davies
Design: Halo Design
Head of Business Development: Emma Wall
Managing Director: Andrew Main Wilson
Chairman: George Cox

Published for the Institute of Directors and KPMG
by Director Publications Ltd
116 Pall Mall London SW1Y 5ED
www.iod.co.uk

Editorial: 020 7766 8910
Production: 020 7766 8960
Sponsorship: 020 7766 8885
Copy sales: 020 7766 8766
Facsimile: 020 7766 8990

© Copyright June 2000
Director Publications Ltd

Price £9.95

The Institute of Directors, KPMG and Director Publications Ltd
accept no responsibility for the views expressed by contributors to this publication.
Readers should consult their advisers before acting on any issue raised.

Copyright

YOURS TO HAVE AND TO HOLD
BUT NOT TO COPY

The publication you are reading is protected by copyright law. This means that the publisher could take you and your employer to court and claim heavy legal damages if you make unauthorised photocopies from these pages. Photocopying copyright material without permission is no different from stealing a magazine from a newsagent.

The Copyright Licensing Agency (CLA) issues licences to bring photocopying within the law. It has designed licensing services to cover all kinds of special needs in business, education and government.

If you take photocopies from books, magazines and periodicals at work your employer should be licensed with the CLA. Make sure you are protected by a photocopying licence.

The Copyright Licensing Agency
90 Tottenham Court Road
London W1P 0LP
Tel: 020 7436 5931   Fax: 020 7436 3986

Apart from any fair dealing for the purposes of research or private study, or criticism or review, as permitted under the Copyright, Designs and Patents Act, 1988, this publication may only be reproduced, stored or transmitted, in any form or by any means, with the prior permission in writing of the publishers or, in the case of reprographic reproduction, in accordance with the terms and licences issued by the CLA. Enquiries concerning the reproduction outside those terms should be sent to the publishers at the undermentioned addresses:

Director Publications Ltd   Kogan Page Ltd
116 Pall Mall   120 Pentonville Road
London SW1Y 5ED   London N1 9JN

©Director Publications Ltd 2000

British Library Cataloguing in Publication Data
A CIP record for this book is available from the British Library
ISBN 0 7494 3450 3

Printed and bound in Great Britain

Contents

INTRODUCTION   **The quick and the dead** 5
George Cox, Director General, IoD

FOREWORD   **Thriving on change** 7
John Eggleston, head of owner managed business at KPMG

1   **E-commerce in the UK** 9
Hamish McRae, associate editor of the Independent newspaper and contributing editor to Net Profit

2   **Developing the potential** 14
Phil Cotton, head of e-business for the owner managed business team at KPMG

3   **Strategies for e-business transformation** 19
Professor Jim Norton, head of e-business policy at the IoD

4   **Business-to-business trading** 24
Marc Beishon, business and technology writer

5   **Marketing online** 30
Martin Chilcott of e-business consulting and development company Proxicom

6   **Creating world-beating web sites** 36
Malcolm Otter and Magnus Lif, usability engineers at global digital communications consultancy Icon Medialab

7   **Customer relationship management** 41
Lucy Jacobs, marketing director of Siebel Systems UK

8   **The truth about security** 47
Robert Coles, head of information security services at KPMG

9   **Understanding new technologies** 52
Andrew Bush, new technologies manager, Sun Microsystems

10   **Regulation** 57
Peter Coles, head of legal risk services at KPMG

11   **The information super gateways** 62
Russ Nathan, chairman and managing director of Romtec

12   **The next five years** 69
Patricia Hewitt MP, minister for small firms and e-commerce; Elliot E Maxwell, special advisor to the secretary for the digital economy, US Department of Commerce

Sponsor a Director's Guide

With more than 50 titles produced, the Director's Guide series is a highly successful business publishing venture

Each guide is produced in conjunction with a major blue-chip sponsor – from Oracle and KPMG to Cable & Wireless and Fedex – and each is sent free to 50,000 individual members of the IoD in the UK.

Director's Guides cover a diverse range of topics – from e-commerce to growth finance, from customer care to management buy-outs. Research shows the series forms a key part of IoD members' business reading, with a high retention value and pass-on readership. The direct benefits to the sponsor include:

- *50,000 individual director-level circulation*
- *Strong position as an authority in its specialist area*
- *Authorship of three chapters*
- *Full co-branding with the IoD*
- *Seven pages of exclusive advertising, including two colour positions on the covers*
- *A reply-paid card bound into the guide, for direct response*
- *3,000 sponsor copies*
- *Broad press coverage*

For further enquiries, please contact
Business Development and Sponsorship on:
020 7766 8555
or e-mail us at busdev@iod.co.uk

Introduction

The quick and the dead

George Cox, Director General, Institute of Directors

For months the business headlines have been dominated by the stock market volatility of internet companies. Collectively, investors are realising that for every internet "winner" there are likely to be several failures. But the frenzied peaks and troughs of internet shares should not detract from the essential underlying fact that e-business represents the most significant change in the business environment in our lifetime.

Given this, it is surprising that few people saw the digital revolution coming – even though the internet is simply the highly predictable merging of technologies that have been advancing for years. History shows that we find it surprisingly easy to forecast the development of technology per se, but remarkably difficult to predict its effects on business and society.

This Director's Guide attempts to clarify the future direction of e-business. It is already clear that business-to-business activity will grow rapidly. The impact on business-to-consumer transactions is more debatable, but the high street certainly cannot compete with the net on cost, range of available products, or convenience. There will continue to be further rapid technological advances, hastening economic and social change. Not all of these developments will be without problems, but e-business is here to stay. The only viable approach for directors is to understand it and embrace it.

It is a world in which companies, new and old, must be imaginative, enterprising and quick to adapt. Those that can couple these qualities with the established virtues of good management and customer-focus will be tomorrow's winners.

The key to business

KPMG
It's time for clarity.

KPMG is authorised by the Institute of Chartered Accountants in England and Wales to carry on investment business.
© 1999 KPMG UK, the UK member firm of KPMG International

Foreword

Thriving on change

John Eggleston, head of owner managed business at KPMG

There is plenty of advice for those thinking of setting up a new dot-com business, but far less is available for more traditional companies wishing to create an "e-enabled" organisation. It is the aim of this guide to provide that guidance and help create a blueprint for the integration of other technological developments that are bound to follow.

More than a web page, more than a delivery channel, the internet is a new way of doing business – e-business. There are equal opportunities for large and small companies, where size doesn't matter, but speed does. Delayed reaction is not an option. It will leave businesses even more vulnerable to competition and will risk losing the faith of existing customers and employees, who will regard it as a lack of "e-literacy".

First, companies must acknowledge that e-business is not a technical, but a boardroom issue. It has the power to generate new sales, improve supply chain management and internal processes. Despite its potential, there remains a great deal of uncertainty about what action needs to be taken. Embracing it will inevitably change a business and open up new areas of risk. For example, e-business means global business – how can a company that has never exported deal with this? How will a significant increase in new orders be dealt with? Can the company cope with being more transparent, both in terms of pricing and behaviour? How will new alliances affect its image? How can company and customer information be protected?.

Operating in the new economy is challenging, but success will be based on clear vision, strong internal foundations and a regular re-examination of strategy, so that a company is able to change and thrive.

Be recognised as a professional director

CHARTERED DIRECTOR
The IoD's Chartered Director initiative ensures directors' continued professional education and development.

CRITERIA
Admission to the profession of Chartered Director is open to all IoD members and Fellows with the requisite qualifications who are able to demonstrate the knowledge and experience required to become a member of the profession and who undertake to observe the IoD's Code of Professional Conduct.

BENEFITS
There are clear personal benefits to becoming a Chartered Director. They are recognised as directors:

- *who have achieved standards of professional knowledge and experience;*
- *who have made a serious commitment to their profession;*
- *who have undertaken to act with probity and honesty.*

The letters *C.Dir* that Chartered Directors may append to their names are an easily recognisable badge of professionalism.

As a condition of continued registration, "chartered" members must commit to Continuing Professional Development (CPD) – at least 30 hours a year keeping themselves abreast of both practical and theoretical developments in direction.

To find out more about becoming a Chartered Director, telephone 020 7451 3210, or visit the IoD's web site at www.iod.co.uk

The IoD is ideally suited to help Chartered Directors achieve their Continuing Professional Development (CPD) requirement.

Look out for this symbol which is displayed on IoD products and publications that can assist directors in achieving their CPD requirement.

Chapter 1

E-commerce in the UK

E-commerce will soon be an integral part of business in countries all over the world. Hamish McRae, associate editor of the Independent newspaper and contributing editor to Net Profit, explains why the UK is better placed to make the transition than most

We are a lucky country. The storm that started in the US and swept across the Atlantic – the e-business revolution – has now shaken most of the world. But, by a set of happy coincidences, the UK looks set to benefit from it as much as any other large economy. The whole world will gain from the radical changes that are taking place in the way countries, companies and, indeed, ordinary individuals operate, but those gains will be felt more quickly in some places than in others.

THE TWO SIDES OF E-BUSINESS

What is e-business? Most people think of it as buying goods or services over the internet – for example, buying a book from Amazon.com. Business-to-consumer (B2C), as it is called, is certainly a crucial part of e-commerce. For the moment, books remain the most frequently purchased item over the net, but purchases of other goods and particularly services are rising explosively too. We are in the early stages of a migration from shops to screens.

At the beginning of 2000, the proportion of total retail sales over the net was still tiny in the UK – 0.8 per cent, half the proportion in the US. But "e-tailing" is already beginning to have an enormous impact on consumer behaviour. It only needs a small proportion of customers to scour the net for the lowest

E-commerce in the UK

price for there to be a massive knock-on effect on all pricing. If US experience is any guide, this will depress prices by something like half of one per cent a year for the next decade.

Fortunately, for the commercial world, the net also enables companies to respond to this price-cutting pressure by cutting production costs. In particular, it provides a much cheaper way to manage relations with suppliers and to curb stocks.

This second aspect of e-business, known as business-to-business or B2B, attracts far less publicity than the B2C side, but is growing faster than its more glamorous sibling. Success in the world of e-commerce is clearly not just about expanding the consumer side; it is also about deploying the capabilities of the internet to improve the efficiency of the production of both goods and services.

AVAILABILITY OF E-BUSINESS EQUIPMENT

How, then, from a British perspective, are these two aspects of e-commerce developing? Comparative advantage in the consumer world will turn on two things: widespread availability of the right hardware – so that companies can reach their customers; and the ability to develop the best software so that customers are enticed to buy. You cannot develop e-business if people don't have the kit. But, equally, to gain a real comparative advantage a company has to use that equipment in the cleverest, most imaginative ways.

The hardware side, naturally, is the easier to measure. As of the beginning of 2000, the main way in which the world is developing commercial uses of the internet is over the personal computer.

On that measure, the US leads the world, with the highest PC penetration of any large developed country. The UK is in the middle of the pack – lower than the US, but higher than most of Continental Europe. But PC penetration everywhere is racing upwards, and while Europe has fewer PC users, it has more people "wired" for the internet through another key bit of "hardware", the mobile phone.

E-commerce in the UK

THE NEW INTERNET "CHANNELS"

In crude terms, Europe has half as many PCs per head of population as the US and half as many again mobile phones. That is largely thanks to the early adoption of the GSM standard, now used by two-thirds of the world.

This raises an intriguing question: will the commercial use of the net develop differently in Europe from the way it has done in the US? In particular, now that the first WAP-enabled handsets are being rolled out, will the mobile phone become the main channel through which e-businesses reach their customers?

WAP, or Wireless Application Protocol, gives access to a simplified version of the internet. Web pages have to be cut down so that they can be read on the small phone screen, but if all you want to do is to compare prices or book a restaurant, that may be fine.

In two years' time, even these limitations seem likely to be swept away, as the third generation of mobile phones come into use. These promise much higher download speeds, larger screens and a host of additional facilities. The technology will almost certainly be adopted globally, but the countries with GSM experience will be better placed to think of ways to package e-commerce opportunities into a form that mobile phone users will welcome. When it comes to the migration of e-commerce to the mobile phone, Europe has a head start.

There is a third way in which people may access the net aside from PCs and mobile phones: interactive television. Here, the UK has two advantages and one disadvantage. The advantage is that it has high satellite TV penetration and is an early user of digital TV. The disadvantage is that it has relatively low cable access (though it is rising) and, for the moment, two-way cable TV looks a promising medium for people who wish to access the internet and don't want the complication of a PC.

So in terms of hardware – the extent to which Britons wanting to buy electronically have the equipment to do so – the UK is pretty well placed by global standards. What about the software? Are British firms using the technology well?

E-commerce in the UK

BRITAIN AND BUSINESS-TO-CONSUMER E-COMMERCE

Here one moves from facts to judgments. It is certainly true that the UK has a number of natural advantages. Speaking English is one. The bulk of the available information is in English, which gives countries where English is the mother tongue, or where it is widely spoken (eg. Scandinavia) a natural comparative advantage. In theory, internet technology may be language-neutral. But in practice English has become the default language of the net.

Intellectual creativity is also enormously important. After the US, the UK is the second largest exporter of services in the world and has the second largest surplus on trade in intellectual property.

One aspect of e-business is that it can ship ideas around the world for free. Anything that can be converted to bits and bytes, from software to a pop video, can be traded internationally at a much lower cost and with much greater convenience than ever before. So the UK has the ability, second only to the US, to create intellectual products that can be distributed over the net.

The third requirement for an internet economy is entrepreneurial zeal, coupled with the cash to back it. It is hard not to be dazzled by the burst of start-ups in Britain over the past 18 months, to some extent countering criticisms that the country has been held back by lack of finance to support good ideas. In the 1990s, the proportion of start-ups was about half that of the US, though it was substantially higher than on the Continent. Now cash is clearly not the problem. (What no-one knows, of course, is how many of the dot.coms will graduate to become substantial e-commerce players. The real test for any new business comes in the first down-turn after the initial boom.)

BRITAIN AND BUSINESS-TO-BUSINESS E-COMMERCE

These three advantages should ensure that Britain remains towards the head of the European pack in terms of retail e-commerce.

But what about business-to-business e-commerce? Here, the evidence is entirely anecdotal. It is easy to see the key objective: to streamline the production process. Lots of large companies are racing to use the net for procurement; many are using it to link with suppliers; many are developing intranets for internal communications and extranets to link with other associated businesses. But it is simply too early to make a judgment as to whether this is being done particularly well. Some companies are world class, but there is no easy benchmark to compare performance around the world.

The likelihood is that the combination of relentless pressure to drive down costs and open information about the way competitors are using the net for business-to-business transactions will power business-to-business development of the net everywhere. International best practice will spread very rapidly, much more rapidly than it did in manufacturing technology: there are no secrets, for this is a world of almost infinite information.

GUARDING AGAINST THREATS

Threats? On paper, the UK seems very well-placed. It is the main English-speaking country in the European time zone and, in commercial terms, it is well connected by its strong record of international investment – both inward and outward. It has a government that is broadly favourable to e-commerce and a prime minister who talks of Britain becoming a global leader in the field. On the other hand, it is also part of the EU, which may be a disadvantage if the European Commission is successful in its efforts to tax e-commerce.

Against this, though, is the fact that the whole distinction between e-business and other business will become irrelevant. There will be no such thing as e-business because all business will be e-business. There is no opt-out: to be a success in any part of the commercial world in the future you have to be successful in the electronic aspects of your business as well as the physical ones.

Chapter 2

Developing the potential

Willingness to change and the ability to create a strategy that does not reverse past achievements are essential requirements in the new order. Phil Cotton, head of e-business for the owner managed business team at KPMG, explains how to meet them

These days, even the ads in the Gents promote web page designers. Using the net now seems almost as natural as using the *Yellow Pages*. But communication through the internet is much more than a web site, more than a distribution channel – it is a new way of doing business. It promises as much for smaller businesses as it does for large organisations. Speed and flexibility of attitude are much more useful weapons than size in this revolution.

The amount of media coverage given to dot com entrepreneurs and the millions they are making has, in many ways, deflected attention from the value the internet holds for the majority of us. If shareholders have triumphed in the first wave of the revolution, then the focus of the second wave is going to be on customers, suppliers and employees.

THE POTENTIAL

Research from the US shows that the internet has the power to deliver between 10 and 20 per cent growth in sales and between 10 and 20 per cent improvements in efficiency, promising greater profits and greater savings.

Companies are striving to capitalise on the opportunity the internet offers to enter new markets and improve supply-chain management and customer service. But they are also struggling to flourish in a world where the competitive environment is changing.

Developing the potential

The internet can improve competitor catch-up time and make it more difficult to sustain advantage. More readily available information makes it easier for customers to compare prices, and those charging higher prices than their competitors will need to justify them.

THE VIRTUAL WORLD

Embracing the internet effectively is challenging. There is a lot of uncertainty in both large and smaller companies about what action needs to be taken. E-business strategies differ from traditional business strategies in that they focus on a new global economy in which the rules of the game have changed or are still in the process of being defined. (See box.)

Some companies are fully e-enabled, adopting the new technology to benefit business-to-business, business-to-consumer and internal relationships. Others have concentrated on one type of relationship, but many more are still watching and waiting.

In a recent study by KPMG, it was clear that a worrying paradox was emerging. Business leaders believe that new and innovative information technology is critical to success, but they cling to the misconception that IT does not contribute to profit and they do not understand how entry into the e-business environment can help their organisation. In today's fast-moving world, further delays in the decision to address the impact of the internet are dangerous. Companies that dither not only allow competitors to get ahead but also run the risk of alienating stakeholders: employees, customers and investors will soon lose faith in a business that they do not consider to be as e-literate as possible.

THE BOARDROOM ISSUE

For e-business to succeed, the internet must be seen as a strategic issue for the board, rather than isolated as a technological issue. Businesses must ensure that there is a clear overall vision of where the business is heading in the virtual and physical marketplace, that the selected e-business strategy is in line with that vision and that a culture of constant improvement through change is adopted. Tax and legal planning should also be considered as part of this process. Getting this strategy right can minimise the penalties paid for non-compliance, make your product more price-competitive and improve profitability.

OUT WITH THE OLD, IN WITH THE NEW

Traditional business strategy	E-business strategy
■ Certain measure of predictability, forecasting business development in one, three or five to 10-year spans	■ Focus on adaptability and responsiveness. Implementation times of three months or less and no predictability
■ One-time development effort	■ Iterative strategic development process, as competitive advantage is very fleeting and pace of technological change very rapid
■ Business strategy very much based on positional power	■ In the electronic marketspace, business strategy is based more and more in access, control and manipulation of critical information. Informational power is key
■ Factory and production of goods the core focus	■ The customer has to be the focus. In the internet economy, the customer is king.

E-ENABLEMENT

The internet has the power to transform a business, but the opportunities that can provide the most value to an organisation are often not easy to identify, requiring decision makers to think the unthinkable, to deconstruct and then resurrect their business. An e-enabled business is a business that is innovative, flexible and prepared to experiment and tolerate failure.

Companies may need to break through traditional, deep-rooted ways of doing things. The need to move quickly will encourage businesses to form partnerships and strategic alliances, previously unimagined. These and other changes open up new areas of risk. Businesses must move quickly but they must not make rash decisions. Making sure rapid change is also sensible change is arguably one of their biggest challenges.

BESPOKE STRATEGY

Before investing in e-activity, it is helpful to appreciate that every company has a different entry point. For some, internet technology might transform a sales function and have wide ranging implications for a number of departments; for others, it might be a sophisticated promotional tool. It is important to establish where the particular value is for you. This means going right back to business fundamentals and re-evaluating your vision, identifying the opportunity and defining the risks methodically to help give the best possible information on which to base decisions.

The future belongs to those who can use the new technology to make themselves more efficient, develop better products and deliver improved service. The results are not as instant as the success of dot com entrepreneurs might lead you to believe and, as with many other investments, it may take some years to get a full return. But you ignore the new technology at your peril.

THE FIVE PARTS OF AN E-PLAN

Strategies for the virtual market place should be built on several common elements

ONE: Vision

- Relevance – the company must have a comprehensive appreciation of what the new technology means to the business

- Change – the company must understand the impact of "e" on the business model and the need for regular review of the business's direction in a faster changing business environment

- Value – the company must know when to expect returns and how stakeholder value can be protected and increased

- People – the company must build competencies to drive the business forward

Developing the potential

THE FIVE PARTS OF AN E-PLAN

TWO: Marketing

- Competitive advantage – understanding of what rivals are doing. Will return on investment be made by capturing market share, reducing cost, extending market reach or improving service?
- Channels – use of web sites, interactive digital TV, bulletin boards, search engines to reach customers
- Product – application of the new technology to help shape an improved product
- Profitability – developing management information on the profitability of individual customers and products
- Brand protection – consideration of whether new alliances will enhance or dilute brand value

THREE: Design

- The web – making sure pages are easy to use, attractive and fast
- Quality control – constant checking of material on web pages for accuracy, topicality and authenticity

FOUR: Operations

- Systems and business process integration – streamlining/redesigning manual processes to make best use of the technology
- Fulfilment and revenue management – accounting for and monitoring transactions and effective collection of monies
- Intermediaries – alignment with appropriate professional navigators to ensure traffic to the site is of the right sort
- Third party – checking that third parties will meet quality, reliability and security standards

FIVE: Compliance

- Monitoring and audit – has there been an independent examination of the service?
- Regulatory – does the business comply with all of the regulations governing e-commerce eg. consumer protection, data protection?
- Tax – where will tax liabilities arise?
- Law – what is the legal position regarding contracts in every country where sales are made?

Chapter 3

Strategies for e-business transformation

The "journey" to the new business world poses new hazards. But the old checkpoints such as customers, competition and costs still apply. Jim Norton, head of the IoD's e-business policy, explains how to plot your course

During 1999, awareness of the potential importance of e-business – both in business-to-business (B2B) and business-to-consumer (B2C) applications – rose dramatically. According to analysts IDC, UK B2B revenues are expected to reach £28bn in 2002 – some four per cent of UK GDP. According to the accountants and management consultants Ernst & Young, B2C may account for 24 per cent of all UK retail sales by the same date.

Many companies are now exploring how e-business tools can improve customer service, reduce inventory, enhance quality and speed up time to market. For most businesses, however, such exploration is only the first step in a process that may ultimately transform the nature of the business itself: it may lead to radically new types of product or service, new means of financing and novel charging methods.

THE RESPONSE OF COMPANIES

How can companies prepare for these further challenges? The key is to complement their detailed knowledge of their own business with awareness of the capabilities created by the "e" element. They need to appreciate and experience the new opportunities that the internet, interactive digital television and third-generation mobile communications offer. Crucially, they need to be able to

Strategies for e-business transformation

relate these new opportunities to the specific requirements of their own business.

E-business is an issue for the board as a whole, not simply for the technologists. It demands full commitment from the top. Successful businesses will be those that have a clear vision and that harness the new capabilities to their business goals. Size will not matter: success will go to the swift, be they large or small.

THE EIGHT C'S

E-business is evolving at a fearsome rate. The commercial map, it seems, is continually being redrawn. But some old business landmarks remain fixed. The eight C's – customers, creativity, co-operation, commitment, charging, competition, culture and cost – should form the basis of strategic planning. The questions the board must ask fall under these eight headings.

Serving customers

The first fixed point is the central importance of customers. The new tools offer new ways of understanding detailed customer requirements. They can bring significant business benefits.

One of the remarkable achievements of e-business has been to "outsource" cost from provider to customer while increasing customer satisfaction through customer "control". Electronic banking by Egg or If and online product specification and configuration by Cisco and Dell are good examples. In online B2C banking, perhaps 99 per cent of the bank's historic transaction cost has been moved to the customer (computer costs, software costs, money paid to Internet Services Providers, telephone charges, time...) yet customer satisfaction has improved. How can you replicate this in your own business?

Creating new value

The next peak in this new business landscape is the creation of value. How can the cascade of information flowing from e-business be used to generate new value for customers, whether other businesses or consumers? Aggregating information (with the customer's permission) can create new opportunities. One example

Strategies for e-business transformation

is the "e-pharmacy". If all of a customer's orders for prescription and non-prescription medicines flow through the same web site, then a personal profile can be developed. Customers will be warned immediately if they are seeking to buy something that may conflict with medications they are already taking. This is new value; more difficult to replicate in the bricks-and-mortar world.

The e-pharmacy's focus is on creativity – recognising the new opportunities that detailed information, gathered at marginal cost can bring. While such a provider may start by offering products at a discount, it will move on to charge a premium that reflects the new value created. What does this mean for your company?

Co-operating with new partners

Although e-business is undermining the role of many existing intermediaries, such as estate agents or travel agents, it is creating many new ones. Such intermediaries, or "infomediaries", can help meet many of the challenges of e-business. They can resolve privacy issues by offering anonymity to consumers, yet also allowing their detailed personal preferences to be made available. They can hold payment in escrow against service or product fulfilment. They can insure transactions and "rate" web sites. They can even, perhaps, help remove key gaps in tax collection for immaterial products such as software or entertainment delivered over the web. In essence, they act to create the environment of trust that is particularly essential for business-to-consumer e-business.

How can your business best exploit these new opportunities? Should it contribute to a sectoral trade exchange bringing together B2B buyers and sellers? Do you need partners or alliances to respond to the global reach (and threat) of e-business? Should you launch an "infomediary"?

Delivering on commitments

A further issue is "fulfilment" – handling all the back office functions well and integrating these seamlessly with the web site. Failure to sort out the back office will guarantee embarrassing failure. Nothing destroys credibility and brand loyalty as quickly as conspicuous inability to deliver on expectations raised. This was amply demonstrated at the end of last year when a variety of web enabled companies sold products enthusiastically but failed to deliver them in time for Christmas; plunging share prices followed.

How can you ensure that your back office systems and delivery networks integrate well with the new e-sales front office?

Charging

Will the way that you have charged for products or services be undermined by e-business? If you have relied on different pricing regimes in different geographic markets, or if you have cross-subsidised one element of your business from another, it is likely to be mercilessly exposed.

The implications are perhaps most obvious in the retail sector. Shops provide value for consumers by allowing them to examine and compare products – without charging them directly for the privilege. Can they survive? What happens if the customer uses them as a convenient "free" showroom, but then buys from someone else over the net (who does not maintain a showroom and thus has lower costs)?

Have you examined your business model to ensure your charging is directly linked to the value offered?

New competition

Will new competitors, perhaps from other countries or other markets, be able to use the power of their "brand" and the lowered costs of market entry to threaten your core business? Could a major brand set up its own web site and deliver products or services into your market? It might simply be an "order taker", relying on your competitors for "fulfilment", yet taking a slice of your business based purely on brand power and trust. How vulnerable is your market?

Culture

Can you manage the transition to the new "e-channels" without provoking conflict with your existing physical channels? Will you accidentally undermine 95 per cent of your existing business in pursuit of five per cent of new e-business? How will you maintain the morale of the team in your "old" business if you are visibly setting up a new e-business to challenge it? Can you build the right mix of people skills and creativity plus technology support? Are you prepared to devolve significant responsibility to relatively junior staff in this fast moving e-world? (If not, you may see many leave.)

Cost

Finally, cost. How can you use the new tools of e-business to push stock back up the supply chain? Can you broaden procurement scope to more sub-contractors and thus drive price down? Can you change the way that work in progress is financed? (Several e-businesses now have a negative working capital requirement. They may be making more on this excess cash than on their core service.)

The above are the key questions for the board. The managing director and his team must be on the bridge steering the ship. Technology adds both immense new engine power and new hazards to navigation, but the board must not relinquish the compass.

Chapter 4

Business-to-business trading

Forget home shopping and customer "interfacing", the best thing about the internet is its ability to cut procurement costs and its potential to transform relationships between companies and their suppliers, says Marc Beishon, business and technology writer

It is the way innovations affect the mass market that gets the most publicity. So these days the spotlight is on "e-tailers" such as online book stores and last-minute travel agencies and the likelihood that, in the not too distant future, you'll be able to access their web sites from your mobile phone.

But consumerism is only part of the e-commerce story. Although growing at a significant rate, the volume of business-to-consumer transactions is small compared with the projections for business-to-business (B2B) electronic trading. Analysts' forecasts vary, but they all point to the growing dominance of B2B in the electronic marketplace: Gartner Group reckons that by 2003 online B2B revenues will exceed $4tn; IDC puts the global worth of goods and services traded to consumers in the same year at $178bn.

By the next year, 2004, B2B should almost double again to more than $7tn worldwide – some seven per cent of all trade between organisations. It's a truly massive market and its growth will inevitably lead to a radical shake-up of trading relationships.

Why is B2B attracting the lion's share of the e-commerce boom? The answer lies mainly in the opportunities the internet has created for improving relationships with business partners and suppliers and the efficiencies and cost-savings that can be made through electronic trading channels. Organisations have been waiting for years for a low-cost, easy way to take the pain out of simple transactions such as the purchasing of indirect supplies.

SIMPLIFICATION OF PROCUREMENT

Relatively complex systems such as Electronic Data Interchange (EDI) are now being swept away by internet-based electronic procurement solutions that are probably the biggest contributors so far to the B2B success story. In many ways, these procurement systems epitomise the key benefits of internet technology, increasing user choice and user "power" while decreasing costs.

British Telecom, for example, is in the process of rolling out a huge e-procurement initiative across all its 60,000 employees. The company spends about £5bn a year on goods and services and issues more than a million purchase orders a year. Cutting the associated administrative costs of this huge spend was an obvious target.

BT's solution is a web site where internal purchasers can scour the catalogues of suppliers and select the best offer for their needs. Employees can also find out which suppliers have items in stock and which have the best delivery terms, and chart the progress of the order from approval to delivery.

The financial benefits are startling. According to BT, the cost of processing a purchase order used to be £70. This was cut to about £50 after various methods to streamline the procurement system; with the new web-based system, though, it is expected to plummet to just £5. But the savings don't end there. The initiative also means that new pricing and service levels are negotiated with suppliers. E-procurement benefits suppliers because they receive orders direct into their own systems, obviating the need for human intervention. Centralising purchasing through approved suppliers with agreed service levels can also drastically cut down on so-called "maverick" purchasing, where staff bypass slow and unwieldy internal systems and buy goods themselves on company credit cards.

THE FALL AND RISE OF THE INTERMEDIARY

As an e-business service provider in its own right, BT has set up this purchasing "portal" for other buyers to participate in, reflecting another strong trend in the internet economy – that of the value-added intermediary.

Analysts have been particularly preoccupied with what e-commerce means for the role of the "middleman", such as the traditional distributor in a supply chain. There was an initial feeling that suppliers would opt for "disintermediation", cutting out distribution channels and going straight to their markets. Highly successful direct selling organisations such as Dell, the PC maker, have made a natural transition to the internet, shifting millions of dollars of equipment each day. Similarly, in Britain, existing and new financial services firms have taken to the net, direct selling theoretically complex products such as mortgages and insurance.

But the wholesale elimination of middlemen does not seem to be happening in most markets. Instead, intermediaries are finding there is plenty of opportunity to add value to the supply chain. They are complementing their traditional roles by offering the information that enables buyers to make purchasing decisions and by providing services that both buyers and sellers need in trading over electronic channels, such as finance provision and local marketing skills.

MODELS OF THE MODERN ECONOMY

Paul Timmers, in his book *Electronic Commerce, Strategies and Models for Business to Business Trading*, says the internet can enable a huge number of business models and identifies 11 that are now in either experimental or commercial operation. They include procurement systems, virtual communities and collaboration platforms, where common interests and tools are pooled, and value-chain suppliers, such as banking and courier services.

Also mentioned are "value chain integrators" – suppliers that use the internet to diversify from their core business. Marshall Industries, an electronic components distributor, for example, has evolved from being just a catalogue operator to a company that offers a range of internet-related products and services. Its "portfolio" now includes: online news and information; online ordering of parts; online discussion with engineers; a language partner providing information in 17 languages; personalised web pages that allow customers to see their purchase history and their own pricing schemes; an electronic design centre; a special service for value-added resellers. As Timmers, says, Marshall has "enriched the intermediation function" and "integrated additional value-chain functions such as payments".

THE NEW BROKERS

Another sort of e-commerce intermediary is the broker of information and consultancy, from the portal-style information web sites that started life mainly as search engines, to consultancy and market research firms offering commercial business information services.

Then there are electronic shops and malls and auction-style sites. While the former are mostly oriented towards the business-to-consumer markets, the latter are also working well in B2B markets. There has been a spate of announcements in web sites that allow buyers of items such as standard computer equipment to post their requirements while remaining anonymous – suppliers that want to bid for the business can then send their tenders with little of the expense normally involved in "pitching" for clients. Meanwhile, the owners of the auction/broker sites pick up transaction fees and advertising.

Timmers adds that these sorts of "e-auction" sites are particularly good for shifting surplus stock.

THE VALUE CHAIN

So these days, the term "supply chain" is being replaced by the more doubled-edged term "value chain". This implies that everyone in the chain has to add value to the process, especially in electronic channels.

The degree of sophistication in the various business models described by Timmers varies widely – electronic shops and procurement systems are lower down the innovation scale, and are less complex, than the type of value-chain integration pioneered by Marshall. But there can be little doubt that all companies that want to get the best out of electronic trading must look at its implications for B2B and the way the supply chain is managed.

According to Paul Baker, head of the electronic commerce

practice at KPMG Consulting, British companies are perhaps focusing too much on internet opportunities with end consumers. "The biggest improvement we see in firms which adopt electronic trading comes as a direct result of the improved communications with partners and suppliers," he says, pointing to the benefits of electronic procurement.

IMPLICATIONS FOR SMALL FIRMS

Some action is clearly imperative for all companies, particularly traditional suppliers. With governments and large purchasers such as BT converting all their buying to electronic channels, it's either join in or die out if you get a lot of your revenue from the big buyers.

And although the development of electronic trading is very much a joint effort at present – virtually everyone involved is a pioneer – smaller firms cannot rely on friendly co-operation for ever.

Market research should take into account both the new types of internet business models and what the competition is doing. The best added value is added value that is different. Don't do your homework and you could find that your new web site for the reseller community is trounced by a competitor also offering, say, a tie-up with a highly attractive finance scheme for end customers. Or you could be beaten by someone offering a superb "personalised experience" for business buyers, with incentives such as extra airmiles thrown in.

THE SUPPLIER "ASSOCIATE"

Companies could do worse than follow the example of the world's most famous electronic business. When Amazon.com, the online bookstore, is discussed, the focus is usually on its consumer shopfront operations, and, of course, its still non-existent profits. But there are also B2B parts of its model that have played a crucial role in taking the company to its near billion-dollar turnover.

First, Amazon Associates provides a way for publishers, authors and virtual communities of any description to link to

Business-to-business trading

Amazon. For example, buying books at C S Lewis's web site is "fulfilled" by Amazon. The company has more than 400,000 such associates signed up in various ways. Then there's the Advantage programme, which allows publishers to merge their catalogues into Amazon's main online catalogue and offers inventory control and revenue sharing.

This is a partners-and-suppliers strategy writ large, and, of course, there are other B2B processes involved, such as the shipping of items and making payments to publishers.

The challenge for all firms is to both build electronic business into existing channels, and, like Amazon, spot models for getting totally new revenue streams. You have to make everyone – from a C S Lewis to a Douglas Adams – work for you. And, no, the answer here isn't "42".

BUSINESS-TO-BUSINESS OPPORTUNITIES

Electronic trading can improve:

- Efficiency: throughout the value chain – from raw material supplier to the end customer – you should look to provide improved product availability and reduce wastage. Aim for: a reduction in cost per transaction; consolidation of the supplier base; value-based pricing with suppliers; a reduction in administrative costs.

- Innovation: electronic channels offer tremendous scope to add entirely new services such as information portals, online auctions and brokerage, and new value-added communities that feed into your business.

- Internal operations: you should provide easy-to-use systems for employees to carry out routine activities such as procurement and look at systems for business partners to help themselves to information and transactions, too.

- Knowledge management: consider applications that allow communities of internal and external personnel to learn and collaborate on new projects, sales training, marketing, market research and so on.

Chapter 5

Marketing online

Online, customers experience messages about a business at the same time as they experience service. This, says Martin Chilcott of leading e-business consulting and development company Proxicom, makes good brand management more important than ever

In the new economy, businesses will only be able to acquire and retain customers profitably in the long term by becoming genuinely customer-centric. Marketing – the way a company communicates with its customers – will therefore be business-critical. It will increasingly be seen as having a primary role in the development of companies.

This chapter focuses on some of the ways strategic marketing can be used to plan, build and roll out successful online businesses. In particular, it will examine the role of the brand as a strategic tool for determining the fundamental nature of an online business and its interaction with its target audience.

IMAGE AND EXPERIENCE

Traditionally, the brand has been thought of as a communications tool, created and managed by corporate identity and advertising departments and agencies. The brand's definition and development have usually been left to the final stages of the roll-out of a "go to market strategy". And brand values have largely been communicated by imagery wrapped around the basic product and service in order to differentiate it from competitors.

In traditional media, it is possible to project a commercially effective brand image that is unconnected with the consumer's experience of the core product. For instance, it is possible for me to love the brand and imagery associated with Guinness and dislike the drink itself. I can be a Guinness lover without being a stout drinker. Obviously, the relative importance of perception over experience changes with product use, but the power of broadcast media is such that brands often retain significant value with consumers despite poor product performance.

Online, brand values are communicated through imagery and experience simultaneously. In interactive media, it is impossible for the brand imagery and the interactive experience to be dislocated and for the brand to still communicate its values effectively.

Imagine a courier company positioned as the fastest deliverer of parcels across the country. If this positioning and the necessary supporting brand values of speed were communicated in writing and imagery, but the web site downloaded slowly, or if customer service e-mails were not replied to for several days, credibility would be lost.

DEFINING THE INTERACTIVE BRAND

For a business to be an effective brand online it has to live up to its values through all dimensions of the interactive experience from content and functionality, through to customer service and graphic design. It is about making a business be true to and integrate with its values, rather than just about projecting an image of those values. This means that the effective communication of brand values through interactive media requires a more inclusive set of disciplines than just marketing communications.

The fundamental difference between interactive and traditional media is the result of the former's ability to be simultaneously both a communications medium and a channel to market: both the means for brands to communicate a promise and for consumers to test that promise.

As a result, an effective interactive brand becomes a means for the business to articulate to the consumer its compelling customer proposition. It makes a promise and it delivers against that promise simultaneously. That being the case, the process of identifying a competitive position for a brand and articulating its values is the key to the process of defining compelling content, functionality, service etc. Defining the interactive brand defines the customer's experience of the business.

RELEVANCE, VARIETY AND INTEGRITY

In examining the experience of brands online, it is necessary to consider:

- *The effect upon the brand of interactive media's bi-directional characteristics;*

- *The importance of web communities;*

- *The challenges of managing a brand in a fragmented medium.*

Bi-directional interactivity enables customers to "personalise" the delivery of brand promises and experience. It enables them to interact one-to-one with brands in a way that is relevant to them, thus making products, messages, services and their delivery more personal. Sophisticated brand web sites engage consumers continuously in a conscious and unconscious dialogue with the brand, through the business's databases. As a result, sites such as Yahoo! and Amazon deliver different messages, content and functionality to different customers depending upon their behaviour, where they have come from, what they have previously bought, their stated preferences and their value, etc.

DIFFERENT BUT THE SAME

"Personalisation" creates an interesting new challenge for brand management: how to balance consistency with consumer preference in real-time. In the online world, effective marketing depends on the ability to make the experience of the brand relevant to a specific customer or group of customers without compromising brand integrity. The method of communication differs but the brand values remain the same.

Let us take our courier company again. Imagine two different users of the company's web site. One logs on through a basic modem and the other through a high-speed office connection. The courier company wants to communicate the same value of speed to both users through the delivery of the brand promise and the brand experience via the web site. But to do this, it must take into account the different connection capabilities of the two

Marketing online

users. It must deliver slightly different content or functionality to each user according to the speed of their connection and the time it takes them to download/send data. If the courier company manages this properly, it is able to customise the delivery of the brand promise and the experience of speed in a way that is optimal for both types of customer. As a result, both users "take out" a sense of speed from interacting with this brand, although they do it in very different ways.

BUILDING BRANDS THROUGH WEB COMMUNITIES

In online communities, customers play an important role in defining the communication of brand values and personality. Of course, interactivity online is not confined solely to communications between brand and customer. The development of virtual communities, of customer-to-customer communications, has become increasingly common within branded environments. The ability to use customers to shape and strengthen perceptions of the brand is another way interactive digital media affect brand development.

Some web businesses have used the views and actions of their customers to create the very essence of their brands' personality and values. The most powerful examples come from the out-and-out community portals such as Third Age and Parent Soup. However, Yahoo, Ebay and Amazon can all claim to have used customer involvement effectively in their sites to differentiate themselves from competitors – Amazon through the use of customer-to-customer advice and recommendations and Ebay through enabling direct customer-to-customer trading.

The dynamics of the online community may be usefully compared with those of the football club. Football supporters perceive the contribution of other fans as being a fundamental component of the brand's personality and value. Even when the core "product" is performing badly, fans remain loyal not just to the team, but to one another and will turn up at matches to meet friends, sing, etc. In strong online communities, members, just like fans, play a considerable role in shaping the personality and values of the online brand and in doing so create significant competitive advantage for the brand itself.

CONTINUING ROLE OF OLD MEDIA

Interactivity necessarily fragments media and creates new challenges for brand development. Interactive, digital media are designed to provide customers with choice: choice of channels, web sites, pages, content etc. The effect of providing choice is necessarily to fragment the audience interacting with any given piece of content. As a result, interactive digital media rarely ever achieve the size of audience of broadcast media. This raises some interesting questions about the role marketers should prescribe for interactive media in the development of brands. Clearly, fragmented, narrow-cast media is less cost-effective at creating brand awareness than broadcast media.

Evidence to support this comes from recent studies of online banner advertising that demonstrate falling levels of brand awareness and falling levels of "click-through" rates. In part, this is ascribed to the difficulty of getting complex brand promises across in very limited space and over limited bandwidth and in part to the counter-intuitive way in which demographically targeted banner advertising interrupts users "engaged in focused online missions".

Take the following example: if I am in the process of buying insurance online because it is relatively quick, convenient and inexpensive, I am unlikely to notice or respond to banners advertising dog food, even if I am a dog owner. At that moment, I am not in the market for dog food. To become interested in dog food would require me to switch "missions" and would detract from the convenience of the web for buying insurance. It is not surprising then, that significant interactive brands on both sides of the Atlantic from Amazon to EasyJet rely heavily upon traditional media to raise brand awareness among both online and offline audiences.

However, the power of interactivity does allow new media to communicate deeper, more compelling brand promises and experiences to highly targeted audiences. Accurately targeting

Marketing online

hot prospects and existing customers with rich interactive brand experiences, rather than just brand promises, is one of the keys to effective brand management today. Another is making sure there is close integration between new and old media: there must be no conflict between the "value" available online and the way it is advertised through traditional print and broadcast media.

FLEXIBILITY AND UNDERSTANDING

In summary, then, interactive digital media have an important role to play in the development and management of brands, but brands communicate their values in subtly different ways online. Interactive media communicate brand values most powerfully through:

- *The simultaneous delivery of brand promises in copy and graphics and of services and products in interactive content and functionality;*
- *The customisation of content and functionality to maximise its relevance;*
- *Engaging customers directly and indirectly through communities;*
- *Close integration with traditional media.*

In an online world, where products and services and the way they are communicated can change rapidly, marketers need to be tremendously flexible, taking into account direct customer involvement, customisation and the power of communities. They will need to focus more on understanding customer perceptions and experiences and less on the mechanical management of graphic brand assets. The effective management of fundamentals such as values, personality and positioning will be the cornerstone of developing effective brands online.

Chapter 6

Creating world beating web sites

Many users leave company web sites frustrated that they cannot find what they need or buy what they want. The solution? Better design. Malcolm Otter and Magnus Lif, usability engineers at the global digital communications consultancy Icon Medialab, explain how to get it

If you want to succeed online you need to have a good understanding of your web user's needs. If users don't like your site, they can soon find another one; your competitors are just a click away. Usability is the key to getting people to stay.

This may seem like common sense. Who enjoys filling out overcomplicated registration forms when they visit sites? Who prefers a great-looking site where the information is hard to find to a great-looking site that is easy to navigate?

But many commercial sites badly fail the usability test. According to Zona Research 62 per cent of web shoppers give up looking for the item they want to buy online. The usual reason is bad design. A recent report by Forrester Research says approximately 50 per cent of the potential sales from sites are lost because people cannot find the information they need.

The commercial impact of this is clear. "A bad design can cost 40 per cent of repeat traffic, half of potential sales," says the Forrester report. There is also the effect on a company's reputation to consider. A web site is an interface between business and customer: get it wrong and you damage customer relations.

Creating a site with high usability is of fundamental importance to all businesses on the web. Usability goals are business goals. Good user interface design does not happen by chance. It starts by analysing the various sorts of information that different users will need and linking them together. Web site design may be a young and immature business, but our knowledge about human behaviour has taught us what works and what does not. At the heart of what works is an appreciation of the user or customer and what he or she wants to do.

HUMAN COMPUTER INTERACTION

Human Computer Interaction (HCI) is a discipline concerned with understanding users and their needs and designing interactive systems that correspond to those needs. It is interdisciplinary, bringing together knowledge from the fields of computer science, psychology, software engineering, linguistics and sociology.

An ever-increasing number of clients realises the need for HCI expertise. A key objective of involving HCI from the start and throughout the development process is to ensure the usefulness and usability of online products. With easy-to-use web sites, users can perform their tasks more quickly and more efficiently, making fewer mistakes and gaining more satisfaction.

WHAT IS A USABLE SITE?

A usable site:

- *Is driven by user needs;*
- *Provides relevant information and services;*
- *Is efficient;*
- *Is attractive and creates a positive user experience;*
- *Allows users to concentrate on performing their tasks (eg. booking a flight, buying a computer etc.).*

A usable site means that:

- *Users are more likely to stick around;*
- *The development time of online business is decreased;*
- *The number of satisfied visitors is increased;*
- *Business objectives are made easier to meet.*

THE BUILDING PROCESS

So how do you get a site that works effectively for you and your users/customers? The answer is to involve HCI consultants as early in the building process as possible – from the moment you know that a site needs to be developed or revised. The biggest problems arise when usability testing comes too late in the development cycle.

The development cycle should be iterative and include a number of different phases:

- *Data gathering;*
- *Data analysis;*
- *Design;*
- *Evaluation.*

The object of the data gathering phase is to gain a good understanding of the target users and their needs. It can involve a variety of methods and techniques:

User interviews

User interviews will capture the data necessary for the design of the site, revealing the information users need to know and how they will use it when performing different tasks.

Competitive review

Understanding what competitors are doing will help ensure a site provides the best solution. It is important to know the state of the art of similar services or systems and how existing users rate what's already on offer.

Client interviews

The client usually has a good understanding of its users – or thinks it does. The HCI consultant will gather as much information as possible from the client about the end-users and compare that with the information gathered during the user interviews. Such interviews can be conducted effectively on either a one-to-one basis or through workshops.

DATA FIRST, DESIGN SECOND

After information gathering comes information analysis. The HCI specialists carefully examine the data, deciding which requirements are most important. By the end of this stage, they should have a good understanding of the user population and be able to produce a document that specifies user requirements.

The results of the analysis are the building blocks for the design or re-design. Basing a site on information that has been carefully gathered and analysed will minimise the risk of getting a design that is incompatible with users' needs.

During the design phase, the HCI specialists work closely with creative experts. The right design evolves in an iterative way. Sites are "tested" for usability. The method of evaluation differs from project to project but two of the most common techniques are expert evaluation and user evaluations.

Expert evaluations

These are performed by HCI specialists to ensure that the site is easy to use and conforms to how people perceive and process information in general. In the course of such evaluations, the structure and design of the site are analysed and potential usability problems are identified.

User evaluations

Potential end users perform a variety of tasks by using a "beta" version of the site. The object is to see how the final version of the site would perform "live".

Meanwhile, HCI specialists observe users and check how well the site corresponds to their requirements. Such live demonstration is thought more reliable a test than focus groups: after all, what people say they do is not always what they do in practice.

BUSINESS BENEFITS OF A USABLE SITE

The total cost of ownership of a usable site is lower than that of a badly designed site. The benefits of cheaper use and higher returns far outweigh the development costs. A cost-benefit analysis can be carried out by measuring the cost of involving an HCI usability consultant against the benefits of:

- Higher user productivity;
- Higher number of visits and return visits;
- Higher number of transactions;
- Lower cost for user support;
- Decreased costs for redesign;
- Decreased number of user mistakes.

These findings do not just apply to e-commerce sites, they apply to all sites where good user experience is essential. Usability is the key to giving your customers excellent service. The new business order is governed by the same principles as the old: to succeed, you must supply something people want and supply it well.

COST-BENEFIT CALCULATION

This is a hypothetical example of how usability increases profits

Before redesign:
- Average 6,500 potential buyers per day on the site
- 62 per cent of users gave up (based on Zona Research figures)
- 2,470 successful purchases per day

After redesign based on usability testing:
- Average 6,500 potential buyers per day on the site
- 25 per cent of users give up
- 4,875 successful purchases per day

Gain:
- 2,405 extra transactions per day
- 2,405 x an average of £10 profit per transaction = an extra £8,778,250 every year
- Extra revenue generated through cross-selling and up-selling

Chapter 7

Customer relationship management

Today's technology means buyers are now able communicate with companies in a plethora of different ways. How can you be sure they receive a single message about customer service? Advanced CRM solutions are the key, says Lucy Jacobs, marketing director, [illegible] Systems

The internet has radically changed the way consumers behave. With infinite choice, the freedom to roam and the ability to source whatever they want, whenever they want, from anywhere in the world, buyers now have greater power than ever before. This marketplace of seemingly unlimited choice is driving a new focus on the needs of customers.

Companies are rushing to deploy e-business solutions that present the latest and most compelling way for a customer to evaluate and select their product and service. But even as they begin to serve the new digital media, they must also continue to deal effectively with their customers through existing channels such as the call centre, field sales force, high-street branch and dealer network. This presents companies with one of their biggest challenges – how to deliver seamless, consistent customer service across each and every channel to market.

THE MULTICHANNEL CUSTOMER CHALLENGE

Chapter 5 emphasised the need for consistency in the new era. The way a web site "performs" must not conflict with company and brand image. Equally, customers must not receive different "messages" about a company from different "touchpoints".

Customer relationship management

Consistency is one of the bases for good customer relationship management (CRM). Without it, the relationship with the customer can disintegrate, added value can be lost; you cannot persuade a person he or she is valued by and known to you if you keep dealing with him or her in different ways.

When a customer can interact with your organisation through a variety of channels, it is clearly more difficult to maintain a relationship as if it were an ongoing, one-on-one discussion and a single interaction. Customers will often research an offer through one channel and complete the transaction through another. This means you must ensure that from whatever point a customer chooses to enter your organisation – whether via the call centre, the showroom or the web – the information and service they receive is of the same high quality.

To achieve this, companies need to ensure that the data gathered from each customer interaction is disseminated to, and shared between, all staff wherever they are located. Only then can companies formulate a complete and ongoing profile of each and every individual customer's specific needs and preferences, and begin to see a single view of the customer.

CRM TECHNOLOGIES

CRM applications have historically helped businesses to gain a clearer understanding of their customers and to target specific activities at those whose loyalty most directly increases company profitability. These solutions have evolved from small-scale sales force automation and customer service tools to integrated application suites capable of addressing every aspect of the relationship cycle.

But the new generation of customer-focused e-business suites have internet technology at their core, enabling companies to implement a multichannel strategy for effectively addressing customer relationships across the entire enterprise. These applications ensure that fresh customer information is available via the desktop, laptop and mobile phone to the head office, the call centre, the retail outlet and the remote sales force.

Information gleaned at every point of contact – for example, customer preferences harvested via the web site – can be made available to be used and re-used at each and every other point of customer contact.

Enabling all sales people to deal efficiently with any customer enquiry or request in this way maximises the opportunities for an organisation to cross-sell products and services and expands the volume and value of business conducted with each customer.

EMPOWERING THE "EXTRAPRISE"

The CRM task is further complicated by the lengthening of the supply chain. Providing the breadth and quality of products and services that today's empowered customers expect, requires companies to form alliances with like-minded business partners that can provide complementary offerings and expertise. Similarly, as the internet squeezes margins, many companies will look to off-load or, to use the established jargon, to outsource non-core functions to trusted service providers.

Inevitably, this means that the dissemination and sharing of customer knowledge must also extend beyond the walls of the enterprise to embrace these partners, service providers and suppliers across both supply and demand chains.

In order to keep inventory costs low, customer-facing e-business systems can be connected from the point of customer contact through to the supplier's warehouse. To give split-second profit forecasts, customer transaction information gleaned at the dealer outlet or web site can be made available to the business. Ultimately, technology-enabled buying systems will allow customers themselves to configure their offer from your own and your partners' products and services.

Technology is the key to managing the supply chain in a way that strengthens customer relations. E-business applications integrate the operational back office and the web-enabled front door, providing a single view of customer activity across all organisational systems and beyond to partners and suppliers.

Customer relationship management

BUILDING AN ONLINE TRADING COMMUNITY

BT Wholesale Services & Solutions, the wholesale arm of BT, wants to become a single source of communications products and services for more than 300 established and emerging UK telecommunications companies. The company is committed to making it easy for customers to conduct business whenever and however they want.

As part of this drive, BT Wholesale has created a new web-based system called e.Co. Using e-business applications to integrate its disparate sales, service, and marketing infrastructure, e.Co is a single, comprehensive multichannel system powered by one central database of customer information.

As well as offering traditional contact channels such as telephone and fax, BT Wholesale customers can now directly access e.Co via the web to see details on products, work orders and service agreements, as well as place orders and view their account status online within a secure, protected environment. The first major implementation, completed in just 12 weeks, is expected to automate nearly 40 per cent of the formerly manual tasks performed by BT Wholesale staff.

"We wanted the flexibility to implement an e-business solution without changing back-end systems. Now our sales force has much more time to up-sell and provide more value, because they have easy access to rich customer profile information," says Fionnuala Morgan-Rees, head of business transformation.

PLACING THE CUSTOMER AT THE CORE OF E-BUSINESS

Those companies that successfully leverage technology and re-engineer their operations as e-businesses are becoming "virtual" corporations, served by a constellation of partners and channels.

By placing customer information systems at the core, these transformed e-businesses will effectively enable each member of the trading community, whether a direct employee or a channel partner, to deal with any customer request and turn every customer interaction into a source of new revenue. And through the analysis of the information gathered from these customer interactions, companies can, in turn, refine and streamline products and services to match changing customer preferences.

Achieving this transformation requires a set of world-class

customer relationship solutions that provides unparalleled consistency of service across a breadth of channels to market. It also requires solutions that can be fully integrated into the business intelligence, logistics, supply chain and knowledge management processes and applications that are driving decision-making throughout the wider extraprise.

Such a transformed business is able to outperform traditional businesses by responding more rapidly to market changes, operating at the lowest possible cost, responding fastest to customer needs and building long-term loyalty and satisfaction. In an era where the buyer holds the power, this ability to keep pace with the customer will undoubtedly be the key to success.

WEAVING A MULTICHANNEL STRATEGY

With operations expanding throughout the UK and Europe, ScudderThreadneedle Investment Services, one of Europe's leading new investment management companies, decided to streamline its operational, marketing and sales processes in order to keep pace with the rapidly growing business volumes it was experiencing.

At the same time, the company wanted to ensure that it maintained – and enhanced – its customer service.

"Our CRM and e-commerce objectives sit together as integral components in our overall strategy to make it easy for all our customers to do business with us," says Dave Carter, the company's Systems Architect.

To provide customers with multiple options for purchasing and obtaining products and services, ScudderThreadneedle has deployed a multichannel solution. This solution now forms the foundation of a call centre operation and an e-business channel aimed at securing customer loyalty by increasing the company's speed of response and providing customers with greater flexibility and choice.

The solution provides all the information a ScudderThreadneedle agent needs to handle any customer valuation or fund-portfolio enquiry quickly and efficiently. As a result, the company has been able to streamline management of its client data, and gain access to more accurate information to compile reports for both clients and financial advisers.

E-business profile: El Celler Catala

THE BARRIER BREAKER

"It's a way to combine two different passions and become self-employed," says Peter Hodder-Williams of the Web-based wine-merchant business he runs from his farmhouse in Catalonia in Spain. For the last two years, El Celler Catala has been shipping local wines to customers of its website. "Now my main market is the UK, but I'm also shipping to Belgium, Holland, and as far away as the Philippines."

At 31, Hodder-Williams had neither experience in the wine trade nor the knowledge of how to trade across national borders before he left his job with the Cambridge University Press for wine and Catalonia.

But the learning curve was not as steep as you might imagine, he says. "Unless you are selling very large quantities to each country you can behave as if you are a national company," he explains. "It's not terribly complicated. I have a euro-based bank account and a euro credit-card terminal, and I use the euro exchange-rate and add Spanish VAT. It doesn't seem to have scared anyone off. The euro is no more frightening than the peseta, and it has a lot less noughts on the prices." But just in case, the site carries a simple explanation of how the euro pricing works.

The practical side of trading across boundaries is taken care of by the hosting service, the Yahoo Store, which provides a basic infrastructure for processing internet transactions and shipping.

UPS shipping, for example, comes as part of the service – customers can log onto the site to find out exactly where their case of wine is in the delivery process. Using a hosting service also means reliability. With no computers to run, costs are low. This has allowed El Celler Catala to grow gradually. Shipping costs can account for one-third of outgoings, but even if it took just one order a day, it would be in profit.

The key to a successful online service, says Hodder-Williams, is to find a niche that only a small company can satisfy. So his fine wines are not widely available even in the rest of Spain, let alone in the UK. By promoting them in specialist publications and on the web, El Celler Catala has found a band of enthusiastic customers that cuts across geographical barriers. He also e-mails his customers a monthly newsletter. Plans for the future include a link-up with a regional ham supplier.

Specialist sites such as El Celler Catala create a sense of belonging more important than physical proximity by building a unique online community that provides what those people really want.

Chapter 8

The truth about security

Fraud, theft, hacking and breaches of confidentiality highlight the hazards of trading over the net. But, says Robert Coles, head of KPMG's information security services in the UK, the risks can be managed to make e-commerce more secure

Press reporting of security breaches over the net, such as hacking and the theft of credit card details, has been widespread. Such coverage fuels fear. In a recent KPMG survey, companies not planning to use the net for commercial services stated perceived lack of security as the chief reason. Seventy eight per cent were worried about fraud, hacking, viruses and threats to confidentiality.

But what the majority of companies do not seem to recognise is that they could implement protection mechanisms that could help develop their business.

As e-entrepreneurs gain more of a foothold in the marketplace, and the consumer becomes more e-literate, involvement in e-commerce begins to look like a necessity rather than an option. Companies can reduce the associated fears by managing the risks.

WHAT THE DANGERS ARE

If you are to develop a risk management strategy, the first rule is to know the risks. The main e-commerce security risks are:

- *Masquerading/spoofing – websites pretending to be legitimate e-commerce sites, individuals pretending to be legitimate customers, employees pretending to be legitimate customers.*

- *Message interception – theft of information, such as credit card numbers and/or modification or duplication of messages.*

The truth about security

- *Message repudiation – denial of a transaction or a message by a customer.*

- *Accidental disclosure of customer information leading to legal liability.*

- *Communications errors leading to loss or corruption of transactions.*

- *Inability to maintain or extend the service due to technology constraints or use of non-industry standard hardware and software.*

- *Code design error or bugs leading to software failure and loss or corruption of transactions.*

- *Hardware failure resulting in the service not being available to customers.*

- *Web server "attack" – denial of service and/or a change of web server content.*

- *Viruses from e-mails or from malicious/fraudulent codes inserted by hackers or internal or external programmers.*

THE RISK REALITY

The risk-list is long, but how seriously should we take it? What are the chances of an incident occurring? While there are very few reliable statistics available, it is important to keep calm. Media coverage has probably distorted the real picture. Common sense dictates that the number of people who deliberately use the internet for fraudulent purposes is tiny: it would be extremely hard to make a living this way.

The odds, then, are in businesses' favour. Many sites with no security do not get abused in any way. But this should not be an excuse for doing nothing. Leaving your site unprotected is about as sensible as leaving your home with the keys in the front door. The financial consequences of an actual security breach are far reaching. There is not just the loss itself to consider, but also

The truth about security

the costs incurred in recovering from the incident and in building more secure systems to prevent further failure. The impact from bad publicity is likely to be even more significant.

REDUCING RISK

Clear-headed assessment of the risks of e-commerce and a strategy to reduce them are, therefore, essential in today's commercial world. However, the KPMG survey found that the majority of organisations do not even meet the British Standard Code of Practice For Information Security Management to cover themselves adequately for the more traditional forms of information risk.

Encryption is not widely used to protect confidential information and if it is used can easily be broken. The security of internet sites is rarely tested and the reporting of security violations relating to external connections is weak.

Twenty nine per cent of those surveyed did not even have the most basic of all controls – a firewall to protect their internal system from "attack" from the internet. Businesses continue to leave themselves wide open to risk. This is for a variety of reasons: sometimes risks associated with technology are not discussed at boardroom level and so the budget available to deal with them is small; sometimes they are simply not fully understood; sometimes, the company knows about them but decides to take a gamble.

RISK MANAGEMENT CHECKLIST

All companies considering or already involved in e-commerce need to implement a risk management strategy and supporting security programme. In developing their strategies, they should ask themselves six key questions:

1. *Is there a framework for security that covers policy, procedures and guidelines and the necessary internal communication to ensure that everyone is aware of their responsibilities?*

2. *Do we have enough trust in our customers and the systems*

to know who has generated each e-commerce transaction? Could we prove this in a court of law?

3 Do we have the hardware and software infrastructure, including firewalls, to provide a first line of defence and strong cryptography to ensure security can be maintained over a public network?

4 Have we made sure that the common routes of attack have been closed off, by testing that our security works in practice?

5 Does everyone know what to do in the event of an attack?

6 Will third parties meet the quality, reliability and security standards that we have set for ourselves?

THE WAY AHEAD

Technological solutions to the new risks that the internet poses are being developed. Public Key Infrastructures (PKI), for example, is a system that can provide privacy, data integrity, authentication and non-repudiation.

Analysts forecast rapid growth for PKI. But advances in security systems, although extremely useful, are no substitute for a long-term strategic solution. It is vital that information, information technology and the associated security risks are recognised as a boardroom issue and not ignored as a bits-and-bytes matter for the backroom. In order to profit from the promise of the internet, the business community must see security as an enabler and facilitator, not an inhibitor.

A business that takes enough care to establish principles for security and embeds them in all elements of the organisation is a business that will reap significant benefits. The investment will provide the basis for identifying, evaluating and managing existing and new risk in a cost-effective manner. More importantly, it will provide increased facilities and functions to trusted users. The future is "e" and those who pioneer its use and make it safer stand a much better chance of making it to the finishing line.

E-business profile: eport

THE NEXT BIG THING

"I'm buzzed up about digital television," says Nick Newman, managing director of eport. "It's like the good old days of the Web all over again."

Newman's enthusiasm is based on his experience of putting together the Formula One merchandising site, GrandPrixInc.com, for US retailer Action Performance, which will also sell merchandise through Sky Digital's interactive TV service, called Open. "It is early days," says Newman. "But the technology is extremely simple. Anyone who has been developing for the Web gets to grips very easily with it."

This is good news for businesses that want to sell on TV, but don't know where to start. Interactive TV has been hailed as The Next Big Thing for the best part of a decade. But now – thanks to separate initiatives from Sky Digital's Open, cable company Cable & Wireless Communications and software giant Microsoft – it is becoming a reality. Last autumn, all Sky Digital customers received Open for free, which offers the chance to shop at Somerfield, Dixons, Next and WHSmith, among others. The other two services are both recruiting smaller retailers that have profited on the Web.

Action Performance's interactive TV site is the same as the website, which generates £2,000 a week of sales. Visitors to the TV site find the interface even more simple than that of the Web, reflecting an overall return to more simple, less graphics-heavy sites, according to Newman. "There is a return to simplicity in the industry as a whole. At our site, you can go in, buy something and get out in six or seven clicks. That's the sort of simplicity you need for television," he says.

At Microsoft, UK Web TV manager Bruce Lynn has been helping businesses experiment with interactive TV. "TV is a simple device. Computers are complex. Good Web design says that if you have 12 items on a menu, cut it to six. In the TV world, if you have six, cut it to three."

Microsoft, unlike Sky Open, is building its Web TV offering using HTML standards – coding used to write Web pages. Lynn believes that this is the only practical way forward, as it allows you to use the same e-commerce site on the Web and the TV.

But even if Newman and Lynn are in different technical camps, they both agree: interactive TV will become even more important for e-commerce than the Web.

Understanding new technologies

Business decisions must be based on what technological change means for the future as well as the present. From the convergence of voice and data communications to dishwashers that "talk to" digital TVs, Andrew Bush, new technologies manager, Sun Microsystems, opens a window on tomorrow's world

We are about to experience a confluence of technological and social change that will rival the Industrial Revolution in scale and importance.

Both the business and consumer worlds are being rapidly reshaped by the impact of the internet and its associated technologies. The way we work, the way we play and the way we interact with each other are all destined to change dramatically. The near future could see everything – even everyday appliances such as dishwashers, washing machines and hi-fi systems – connected to the same ubiquitous network.

Sun believes that what tomorrow holds can be summarised by Four A's: "Anyone, from Anywhere, at Anytime, on Anything". It is now understood that networking has become pervasive and that people should be able to have access to information regardless of expertise, location, time and access device.

Through the deployment of technologies such as the programming language Java and the connection technology Jini, software applications can be delivered to any device; with ubiquitous networking, that content can be delivered anywhere, at any time, and to anyone. For individuals, this provides the ability to access data and applications from many types of equipment. No

Understanding new technologies

longer is the data trapped on one machine; nor is the user limited to the application installed on his or her local system.

IMPLICATIONS FOR INFRASTRUCTURE

The level of service implied by "anytime" requires an infrastructure as reliable as today's telephone network. To handle the huge numbers of transactions that will be generated by the plethora of totally new, and perhaps presently unforeseen, access devices, this infrastructure will need to scale beyond anything we imagine today.

Getting access to the internet will have to be as easy as picking up a telephone. We have come to expect "dialtone" when we pick up a telephone handset in almost any country that we visit. Dialtone already fits the Four A's model, with anyone being able to phone from anywhere at anytime on any phone. In the new world, "webtone" will have to be just as ubiquitous, just as reliable – but from a number of devices, not just the telephone.

THE NEW ACCESS DEVICES

The tremendous growth in internet use will be partly driven by the availability of new access devices. Until now, the PC has been the main internet access device, both at home and at work. Over the next few years, a wide range of other tools for accessing the internet will emerge. These are likely to include "thin clients" (which use the network to find programmes that are then run locally), public kiosks, set-top boxes and, perhaps most importantly, data-enabled digital telephones and other hand-held devices.

Whether it is provided from a personal digital assistant (PDA), WAP (Wireless Application Protocol) mobile phone, screen phone, public kiosk, PC, workstation, set-top box or laptop, access to the internet and the world wide web will become an essential business tool.

But what of the domestic consumer? Over the next 10 years, it is likely that almost every household and business device will have intelligence built-in and will be seamlessly and easily networked together using emerging technologies such as Jini. A wireless network connection using Jini will make this possible;

so a dishwasher, for example, could identify itself to a digital TV in order to communicate via the television screen that it had finished – or that it hadn't been turned on.

SMART TECHNOLOGIES AND CUSTOMER SERVICE

Recent technology agreements with major manufacturers such as Whirlpool, Sears, Bosch and Sony demonstrate that the age of the smart consumer appliance is not far away. A broad range of companies now participates in industry bodies and standards groups such as the Digital Video Broadcasting consortium (DVB), the Open Services Gateway initiative (OSGi), Home Audio Visual Interoperability (HAVi) and Global Systems for Mobile Communications (GSM) to agree the adoption of technologies such as the Java platform into product development specifications.

The rise of "proactive" smart consumer appliances has clear implications for the way energy is used and business is done. A utility company could programme your dishwasher to come on during off-peak times only, giving an additional power discount and balancing power generation; the manufacturer of the dishwasher could be remotely informed of a problem and arrange for an engineer to come when he's next in the area and fix it.

New and emerging technologies are transforming business-to-consumer relations. Companies have access to consumers through a multitude of new channels, such as digital interactive broadcasting via satellite, terrestrial and cable networks, targeted advertising, both physical and virtual, and have far more opportunities to interact with them. The continued explosion in mobile telephony (one billion handsets forecast by 2003) will have a massive impact on these channels, creating the ability to deliver really customised and targeted services to a huge number of users.

PUTTING THE PC IN ITS PLACE

The concept of the webtop, your virtual desktop, delivered to the most appropriate platform, without the need of user-installed software, which restricts flexibility and considerably increases support cost, epitomises the Four A's principle; it gives you the

Understanding new technologies

choice of using the most appropriate access device whenever and wherever it is required.

Press and analysts have begun to herald a new era, in which the PC will not be the dominant platform. By 2002, the majority of network access devices will be made up of a mix of platforms, such as the TV, screen phone, mobile phone/smart phone and PDA.

However, the PC will not go away, any more than mainframes or minicomputers have. It will remain a popular mechanism to access the net, but it will be overshadowed, by orders of magnitude, by more different architectures that support many different access device types.

WHAT TOMORROW'S WORLD WILL LOOK LIKE

Sun's strategy is to enable the Four A's vision to become reality. It has made a number of predictions about how the business landscape will change. The future, according to Sun, is one where:

"Webtone" is as reliable as "dialtone"

The ability to access the net at all times via your webtop is taken for granted. (Wide area network bandwidth is already doubling every six to nine months. It is now possible to send five trillion bits of data per second down a fibre optic cable the size of a human hair. This is equivalent to 70 million people surfing the web via modem at once.)

Networked devices proliferate in number

There is a "network appliance device explosion", as devices including WAP mobile phones and personal digital assistants become cheaper and easier to use. Fast networks connecting smart devices are becoming the norm. It is easy to see a time when anything that uses electricity is networked.

The "infomediary" rules

Individuals are able to get the information they need, wherever they are, thanks to the availability of "personal portals" on the net. Sun's StarPortal and iPlanet Webtop, for example, enable network delivery of Sun's office productivity suite "StarOffice" to any device.

WHAT TOMORROW'S WORLD WILL LOOK LIKE

Standards are uniform
All applications are written to open network standards, which enable any device to communicate with any other.

The networked enterprise meets the networked consumer
The world of business has converged with the networked consumer, who has access to the net 24 hours a day, seven days a week. Costs are driven down; the availability of the access technologies increased.

Scalability is all
The explosive growth of the internet, e-commerce and of "dot-comming" a business means all the rules of availability have changed. The internet has offered unprecedented opportunities, but has also brought unpredictability; the way networks are managed has been forced to change; a new approach and mindset have been needed. Using robust systems, with the ability to provide maximum scalability, is crucial to business performance. Scalability has been redefined: a system is now only considered to be scalable if you can add resources without adding complexity.

Everything is mission-critical
Networked systems must be available 24 hours a day, 365 days of the year. No backup window exists any more. System availability and reliability are paramount.

New service providers are emerging
A new breed of service providers is changing the way businesses are run. We increasingly get our non-core business functions from application service providers. This enables us to lower costs and focus on running the business rather than "running the technology".

Chapter 10

Getting to grips with regulation

E-business is a potentially risky business. How can companies be protected against criminals and hackers? Peter Coles, head of legal risk services at KPMG, looks at recent developments in internet security law

Is e-commerce a legal minefield? At first sight, the answer is yes. E-traders expose themselves to the global legal framework and therefore global liabilities. But legal developments cannot, for the most part, keep up with the pace of change in cyberspace. This creates scope for much confusion. In practice, however, most of the conventional laws apply. The challenge is applying them from a new perspective to a new medium.

This chapter can't cover all the areas of law that should be considered when entering the world of e-commerce, but will concentrate on those relating to internet security issues.

An unprotected internet site is not a secure place to do business. Confidential information can be intercepted by unwanted third parties; hacking and computer "vandalism" are becoming more common. In order to make communications secure, it is necessary to send information in coded or encrypted form. The sender and the recipient need to have corresponding keys to the encryption code to enable the document to be read. In essence, the sender encrypts the document with one key and the recipient decrypts it with another or duplicate key.

APPROVAL SCHEME FOR CRYPTOGRAPHERS

Security is one area where internet law is developing fast. The thrust of much of the legislation throughout the world has been to establish a legislative framework for the encryption process in

Getting to grips with regulation

order to boost user confidence in the security of the net. In the UK, the Electronic Communications Bill received royal assent in April.

Part I of the Electronic Communications Bill establishes an approvals scheme for businesses and other organisations supplying cryptography support services. It provides for a statutory scheme to register cryptographers.

Initially, the approval process was to be administered through a government body. However, due to industry pressure, the statutory scheme has been replaced by a voluntary business-led scheme.

The business-led scheme is being drawn up by the Alliance for Electronic Business and is known as the "T Scheme". The government will not enforce Part I of the Act while it remains satisfied with the effectiveness of the T Scheme.

PAPER VERSUS ELECTRONIC SIGNATURE

Part II of the Bill makes provision for the legal recognition of electronic signatures on documents and the use of electronic communications or electronic storage of information as alternatives to conventional paper use. Documents with electronic signatures will be admissible in court as evidence, but it will be up to the court to decide how much weight should be given to the signature in the light of all the evidence.

There is a large amount of legislation that requires the submission of information in paper-based format. The Bill provides for powers to amend such legislation to allow data – such as filings to Companies House – to be submitted electronically.

The Electronic Communications Bill is consistent with, and seeks to implement, certain provisions of the EU Electronic Signatures Directive, which was published in March 2000 and is intended to harmonise European law on electronic signatures. The Bill is also broadly similar to the EU proposed Directive on Certain Legal Aspects of Electronic Commerce in the Internal Market, which seeks to remove barriers to the development of e-commerce within the European Union.

REVISIONS TO THE DATA PROTECTION ACT

The internet provides an extremely powerful channel for transferring data. This means that the information highway contains vast amounts of confidential information.

Fears that personal data could be exploited, for, among other things, cold selling, has led to the EU Directive on Data Protection and, as a result, a revision of the Data Protection Act in the UK. The Act sets out strict principles and criteria for the obtaining and handling of personal data held by organisations. This provides a degree of protection against personal data held by organisations being misused.

BIG BROTHER FEARS

Personal data is, not however, protected by some kind of confessional seal. In certain circumstances, it can be enforcably disclosed. Much attention has been paid to the government's attempts to give itself the power to intercept digitally transferred information. During its consultation process, the Electronic Communications Bill received a great deal of criticism for providing powers to investigative bodies to access encrypted data. The government withdrew these provisions but they have been embodied in the Regulation of Investigatory Powers Bill, which was introduced to the House of Commons on February 9, 2000.

The Bill repeals the Interception of Communications Act 1985 with a view to bringing legislation into line with advances in communications since 1985. It provides for the interception of communications, a statutory basis for authorisation of covert surveillance by law enforcement agencies and gives powers to law enforcement agencies to access encrypted data.

Part III of the Act provides that a person with the "appropriate permission" can serve notice on an encryption key holder to disclose the key if this is deemed to be:

- *In the interests of national security;*
- *For the purpose of preventing or detecting a crime;*
- *In the interests of the economic well being of the UK; or*

> - *Likely to be of value for purposes connected with the exercise or performance by any public authority of any statutory power or duty.*

"Appropriate permission" is that obtained by a circuit judge (in the UK), a sheriff (in Scotland) or a county court judge (in Ireland).

How the Bill develops through parliament remains to be seen, but it may be criticised for its potential to invade individuals' rights of privacy.

PENALTIES FOR HACK ATTACKS

Computer hacking is becoming an increasingly prevalent activity and one that all organisations need to be aware of. As e-commerce technologies develop, so do hacking technologies. "Even though we have markedly improved our capabilities to fight cyber intrusions the problem is growing even faster and we are falling further behind," FBI director Louis Freeh has said.

The Computer Misuse Act 1990 was introduced to combat the rise in hack attacks. Under section 1 of the Act a person can be prosecuted if he causes a computer to perform any function with intent to secure access to any program or data held in a computer, if the access he intends to secure is unauthorised and if he knows at the time he causes the computer to perform the function that that is the case. The two crucial elements in bringing a successful prosecution are to show the actus reus, ie. that the misuse or hacking actually took place, and the mens rea, ie that the person intended to gain unauthorised access. The mens rea element is the harder requirement to satisfy.

The section is broadly defined to cover all types of hacking activity. Section 2 of the Act goes further and provides that an offence is committed where there is an intention of committing a further offence. There is no need for the offence to actually take place, mere intention is enough. Thus if a hacker gains access to an encryption key with a view to accessing a third party's bank account, he is likely to be liable for offences under sections 1 and 2, even if he doesn't get what he wanted.

Getting to grips with regulation

LEGAL LOOPHOLES?

But does the Computer Misuse Act go far enough? In February 2000, there was a number of denial of service attacks against some of the major companies in the e-world. These attacks caused disruption to Yahoo, for example, for three hours. The attacks took the form of a co-ordinated bombardment of requests to the relevant server. Reportedly, one gigabyte of information every second attacked Yahoo's servers. Given that Yahoo normally copes with a delivery of 465 million web pages every day, this was disruption on a massive scale.

Although this was a severe attack, it is not certain that it would be covered under section 1. There was no unauthorised activity and there was no intention to secure data. There would be grounds for bringing a tortious claim against the hacker but whether Yahoo could rely upon the Computer Misuse Act is open to argument.

As hack attacks develop in sophistication, current criminal sanctions, although broadly drafted, may start to look like anachronisms. The law-makers are waking up to the new developments in e-commerce, and it is fair to say that our current laws and regulations should be adaptable to the new commercial medium, but there will be a period before technological and legal developments are fully inline in the online world.

Chapter 11

The information super gateways

E-procurement portals, which direct users to web sites where they will find what they need, will be central to the development of online business. Russ Nathan, chairman and managing director of Romtec, examines their role

Communities that associate for the purpose of buying and selling are nothing new. The concept of a market for buyers and sellers, usually in a geographical catchment area, has existed since man moved from self-sufficiency to collective production. From quite early civilisation, just about any human need has been satisfied in local, national and international markets.

Communities of buyers and sellers have now traded in everything from farm produce, animals and jewellery to household goods, auto parts, stocks and commodities. Buyers have been both consumers and businesses.

So why is a "web community" something different? The most obvious answer is because the interface between buyer and seller is new. The traditional human exchange, both visual and vocal, has been replaced by an electronic dialogue enabled by the internet and a new generation of IT tools. In practical terms, this requires the buyer to have access not only to some form of currency but also to some kind of technological "hardware" – today, a PC with a keyboard and a mouse, tomorrow a mobile or digital TV screen.

THE "NEW" SHAPE OF CUSTOMER SERVICE

Is the electronic interface a change for the better or the worse? Certainly, it alters the nature of the relationship between buyer and seller. Online, buyers do not see the person they are buying from, do not physically examine products and do not try them out before buying. But the death of old trading values and an erosion of trust between buyer and seller are by no means inevitable. Better information at the point of sale will increasingly enable better judgments to be made about what product best meets the buyers' needs.

THE POWER OF THE E-PROCUREMENT PORTAL

A new community has been created that presents an array of products and suppliers to the buyer. The "e-procurement portal" is an intermediary, a gateway web site to a wide range of products, alternative brands and suppliers. It provides seamless access to multiple web sites.

The positioning of an e-procurement portal is potentially very powerful. Power will be proportional to the number and importance of the customers served, as well as to the network of suppliers engaged. Neither customers nor suppliers can be "owned" since both will wish to remain free to choose; however, portals that are early in to each marketplace and perform well for buyers and sellers will achieve significant market shares. The business model that empowers a portal is illustrated below.

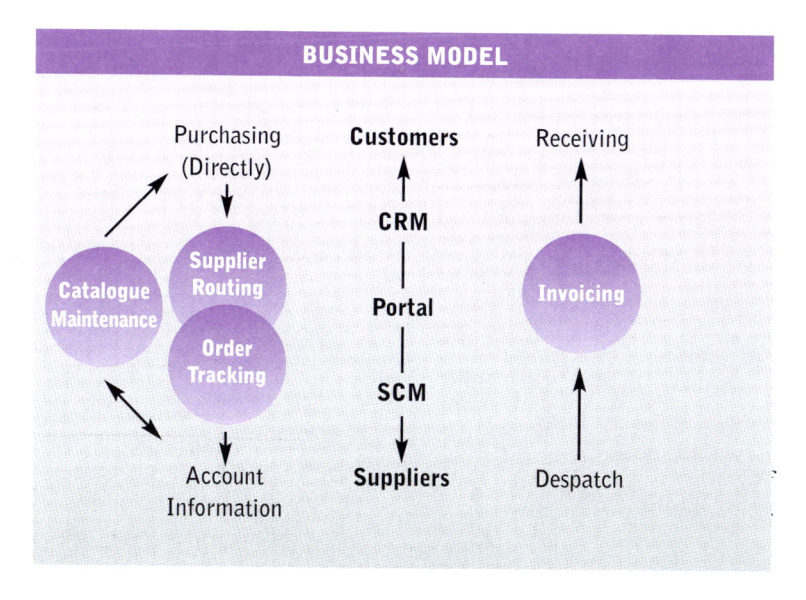

BUSINESS MODEL

Purchasing (Directly) → Supplier Routing / Order Tracking ↔ Catalogue Maintenance ↔ Account Information

Customers ↑ CRM | Portal | SCM ↓ Suppliers

Receiving ↑ Invoicing ↑ Despatch

The information super gateways

PORTAL BUSINESS MODELS

Three kinds of organisations have established e-procurement portals:

- *Intermediaries, usually IT/telecoms services, financial services or distribution companies that have recognised that there is a need to e-enable their, or their customers', routes to market and to participate in a major business opportunity. Current examples include BT, Computacenter, Barclays and Misys.*

- *Supplier groups, which calculate that they can achieve greater performance in their joint target markets by forming alliances. Current examples include: Boeing/Lockhead/BAe/Raytheon; Tesco/M&S/Kingfisher; Sainsbury/Sears/Carrefour.*

- *Major, often global, companies that want to operate a "closed portal" that connects their network of approved suppliers.*

PORTAL ENABLEMENT

E-procurement software is a vital component of each of the three portal business models. Independent software vendors (ISVs) such as Oracle, Commerce One, Biomni and Ariba are playing a decisive role. Beyond software provision, many portals have alliances with telecommunications companies, internet services providers, call centres and delivery companies.

HOW PORTALS BENEFIT BUYERS

Potentially, portals do great things for their founders. What do they mean for purchasers? Benefits for the end consumer include:

- *Convenience of "armchair purchasing";*
- *Savings on travel expenses;*
- *Reduced prices, perhaps as a counter to "rip-off Britain";*
- *A wide range of choice.*

Benefits for the business buyer include:

- *Reduction of overspending;*
- *Reduction of duplication and inventory;*

- *Elimination of "maverick buying", where people in procurement departments choose non-recommended/approved products and services and suppliers, avoiding correct purchasing procedures;*
- *Increased discounts;*
- *Reduction of purchasing costs;*
- *The ability to base buying decisions on up-to-date information.*

(See chapter 4 for a fuller account of the way e-procurement decreases costs and improves efficiencies in companies.)

LIMITATIONS ON PORTALS

Despite their strategic opportunities, portal companies are bound by the limitations of an electronic interface. They will have to recognise these and find ways to compensate for them. The relationship limitations will need to be addressed with effective customer and supplier relationship management (CRM and SCM) systems that personalise buying and selling activity according to individual profiles accumulated from previous transactions.

Automated responses can in most portals be progressed to e-mail communication and, in times of special need, deferred to a "call me" button to obtain a human response.

The limitation set by lack of consumer/client confidence is potentially more difficult to address. The problem, however, is proportional to the amount of money being paid and the degree to which the item being bought is commoditised. People are naturally reluctant to buy very high-value goods or those requiring customisation online but have fewer inhibitions about ordering already trusted brands and making repeat purchases. Purchases that are low value (relative to buyer prosperity) are seen as low-risk.

If they are to convince more customers, e-businesses will have to manage their interface well. This is one of the reasons why web site design is so important (see chapter 6). The "accessibility" of the supplier potentially broadens the scope for uninhibited purchasing.

The information super gateways

BUSINESS-TO-BUSINESS TRADING: BIOMNI

Biomni is a business-to-business e-procurement community. Its launch in November 1999, as a 50/50 joint venture between Computacenter and Computasoft, marked the culmination of almost a decade of development of a now extensively tried and tested e-procurement system

Computacenter, the UK'S largest IT reseller, commissioned e-commerce software specialist Computasoft to develop On-Trac in 1991; by the end of the 1990s the system was being used by more than 400 Computacenter customers and handling about 40 per cent of the company's orders worth £500m of sales.

The launch of Biomni marked the availability of what started as a proprietary e-procurement system for a wider range of products and suppliers. A catalogue of more than 60,000 items ranging from laptop, desktop PCs and servers through modems and peripherals to consumables is being extended to include items such as as furniture and stationery and company cars. Computacenter is just one of the IT product and service suppliers contracted.

Typical buyers using Biomni are corporate customers in the UK, France, Germany and Belgium. Purchasing procedures are tailored to conform to approved products, trading terms and approval rules. Customers include Boots, Greenwich NatWest and UK government departments.

Biomni currently targets large corporate and government organisations that purchase or supply high volumes of operating resources, but it intends to begin marketing to medium-sized business in future. More than 1,500 organisations and government departments are trading over the Biomni network through Directa and customer-specific portals operated by Biomni (including G-CAT, CCD Express, and ICG). An average of 1,400 transactions an hour pass through Biomni's Connecta hub during normal business hours.

Biomni's network currently operates in the UK, France and Germany. There are more than 330 organisations using Biomni's e-procurement software internally and 235 using an internet "shop" or "Lite" version of the software sponsored by Computacenter. A further 700 organisations order goods and services through G-CAT, 365 through CCD Express and 14 through ICG portals. Users of Directa include approximately 27 companies in the FTSE 100.

The information super gateways

BUILDING TRUST

Perspectives on relationships vary distinctly between consumer and business purchasers, and between ad hoc and regular purchasers. Regular purchasers may feel more secure through the provision of a club or subscriber agreement, or simply because regular satisfactory transactions build confidence anyway. In the business-to-business world the relationship is likely to be secured by a formal contract between parties that either have a previous trading history or have taken advantage of professional assessment and reference.

THE PORTAL IN PERSPECTIVE

Of course, not all purchasing activity on the internet is conducted through a portal. More numerous are the "dot.coms" that deal mainly in the products and services of one supplier, for example, those selling tickets for a single airline, railway or theatre.

There are also dot com web sites that provide information on a wide range of products and suppliers but do not accept orders or fulfil them; such operations are referred to as "infomediaries".

Common to both portals and dot coms is the need to fulfil customer-service promises. This brings us back to the similarities between the "new" buying-and-selling communities and the old. Misinform customers and clients about what is available, when it will be delivered and what it will cost, and you risk losing their business – just as you always did.

BUSINESS-TO-CONSUMER TRADING: WHICH? ONLINE

It was in 1995 that the Consumers Association became aware of the demand among Which? subscribers for product and service buying information on the internet

The original objective of Which?OnLine was to make the consumer purchasing information available in their four magazines and numerous publications available to subscribers on demand, wherever they happened to be.

BUSINESS-TO-CONSUMER TRADING: WHICH? ONLINE

A further aim was to offer additional benefits such as integration and searching of all Which? information together with daily updates and news.

In November 1996, the original website was relaunched as a portal site, taking subscribers from selection to purchasing. As is the case for any portal, this required a network of approved suppliers to be established, and maintained.

Today nearly 600 Which? Web Traders belong to the portal including such names as EasyJet, BarclaySquare, LastMinute, Jungle and a host of lesser known SME suppliers. Traders are not charged membership or commission, thus preserving the independent position of Which? Should consumers be dissatisfied traders are asked to remedy any problems. And, ultimately, traders who abuse the Web Trader code of practice at an unacceptable level are struck off.

Which?OnLine is now one of the top 20 most visited websites in the UK; between 50,000 and 100,000 unique visitors log on to the site daily.

Chapter 12

The next five years

What will be the key trends and changes facing those engaging in e-business over the next five years? Two influential figures – Patricia Hewitt in the UK and Elliot Maxwell in the US – give their opinion on the shape of things to come

A UK GOVERNMENT PERSPECTIVE

Patricia Hewitt MP, minister with responsibility for small firms and e-commerce

Most scenarios of the future of e-commerce are determined not by technological progress, but rather by the speed of adoption. In other words, the incredible advances which have been made – mobile telephony, digital television, tiny chips and ever faster processors – are taken for granted, as is the development of better, faster and cheaper content.

But we underestimate the importance of technological advances at our peril. The second wave of the internet revolution will be driven by the need to embed intelligence in products so that they can communicate with each other and to transform digital technology into an integral part of our daily lives. We are seeing this already through WAP – enabling people to use mobile handsets for data exchange as well as talking to others. Further developments will see "things that think" – and things that talk to each other.

This government is working hard to ensure we are ready to catch the "second wave". The UK will be the first country with a relatively high bandwidth communications infrastructure through the auction of the third generation radio spectrum, which will provide an excellent platform to roll out new services and will position us well in our bid to become the best place to trade online.

However, in another sense, the scenarios are right – it is the needs and wants of individuals and businesses that will largely determine how fast and in what direction e-commerce will develop. That is why as "e-minister", I see my priorities as making sure that the economic and social climate enables people to use the new opportunities without barriers and with confidence.

And that includes government itself. For business and government in the next few years making use of the internet will not be an optional extra, but rather an integral part of how we work. Businesses are using the internet to refocus their activities and supply new services, when, where and how the customer wants them. Government is doing the same. You have a right to expect more reactive and more accessible government services over the next five years.

Government has a clear role to play here. Not by dictating and controlling, but by enabling and empowering businesses to use the new technology to its full potential. The UK is already a world leader in the information age, and the government has a target to be the best place in the world to trade online by 2002. We want to work in partnership with business do to this, but ultimately it is business that will make this happen. I therefore encourage all directors to respond to the challenges that e-commerce is laying before us.

VIEW FROM THE US
Elliot E. Maxwell, special advisor to the secretary for the digital economy, US Department of Commerce

Steep declines in computer processing and memory prices have combined with the rapidly expanding capacity of telecommunication networks to propel the world forward into the internet age. During the past five years, we moved from the age of the internet as a technical marvel, to the age of the internet as a business tool. And now we are quickly moving into

The next five years

the age of the internet as a business imperative. As Andy Grove, chairman of Intel has put it, in five years' time all companies will be internet companies, or they will not be in business at all.

The ability of digital networks, such as electronic data interchange (EDI) systems, to generate efficiency gains has been known for decades. However, it was only in the last six years, with the development of browser technology, that we first caught a glimmer as to how the internet, with its open, non-proprietary protocols, could serve as the platform to make these benefits available to businesses of all sizes. And these EDI-type efficiency gains are only one aspect of the transforming power of digital networking. Businesses are exploring new ways of communicating with their customers and negotiating with their suppliers. They are also thinking of new ways to utilise the power of networks in their internal business processes.

In this new network environment, where intelligence exists in a distributed form, innovation is thriving. New products and services are being developed at a rapid pace and new business models are emerging. Firms are reaching new customers and entering markets that previously were unavailable to them. Already, we have seen the development of new online market spaces and the spread of dynamic pricing schemes. Even at this early stage, it is clear that the very terms and categories we use to describe economic activity must be rethought.

During the next five years, we will see further refinements in how we do business. We are likely to realise even more fundamental changes – perhaps nothing less than a reordering of the existing industrial structure. With the development and adoption of more advanced communication protocols (for example, XML), and the growing availability of bandwidth and more sophisticated applications software, companies will be able to bind themselves seamlessly together and just as easily to disentangle. Goods and services that, until now, have been provided in a bundled form, such as banking or insurance services, will now be able to be provided separately. Distinctions between manufacturers, wholesalers and retailers will erode.

The next five years

Firms will have considerable freedom to choose the parts of the value creation network in which they want to compete.

With these remarkable changes also come many challenges. Every business person should be examining how these technologies can lead to new opportunities or provide new competitive threats. While some of today's successful companies may also occupy similar positions five years from now, it will not be because they are producing the same product in the same way. Policymakers, too, need to adapt. The potential rewards to be gained from businesses becoming e-businesses are too important to be thwarted by shortsighted public policies. Given the global nature of e-commerce, it is imperative that nations work together to develop appropriate policies for dealing with important issues such as privacy, consumer protection, and security, in order that both businesses and consumers find the internet a "clean, well-lit" place in which to conduct business.